BREAKING

WITCHCRAFT

BARRIER

AGAINST

FAMILY GROWTH

TELLA OLAYERI

08023583168

Published By:

GOD'S LINK VENTURES

Email tellaolayeri@gmail.com

Website www.tellaolayeri.com

US Contact
Ruth Jack
14 Milewood Road
Verbank
N.Y.12585
U.S.A. +19176428989

DEDICATION

This book is dedicated to the **HOLY GHOST** for inspiring me to write this eye opener book.

APPRECIATION

My appreciation goes to my dedicated wife, **MRS NGOZI OLAYERI,** who typed the manuscript of this book and design the cover page.

My darling wife I say thank you. My appreciation equally goes to my lovely children, **MISS IBUKUN, DAVID, MICHAEL, COMFORT and MERCY.** They encouraged me day and night as I write this book. Hurray, after seven years of research, reading, listening to counsels and support of the Holy Spirit etc. the long awaited book, bad dream enemies use to rob blessing and the way out is out!

Respect and honor should be given to who is due. Favor comes from God and men as well. My calling (writing evangelism) met the timely support of a particular man of God, preacher, teacher, prophet and General Overseer. He awakes my inner man, gave me sound spiritual support and stood by me in fulfillment of my calling.

This book you are holding is a testimony of my claim. This book wouldn't have seen the light of the day, if not for the spiritual encouragement I gathered from my father in the Lord who served as spiritual mirror that brightens my hope to explore my calling.

I am talking of no any other person than the **General Overseer of *MOUNTAIN OF FIRE AND MIRACLES MINISTRIES WORLD WIDE*, DR. D. K. OLUKOYA.**

Once again, I say thank you sir. Your support has yielded yet another earth shaking book.

THANKS

Evangelist Tella Olayeri.

PREFACE

This book talks about, breaking witchcraft barrier which is a tough spiritual assignment a family does. Witchcraft barrier is a tough nut to break, but God being on your side, you shall overcome it. Witchcraft barrier is a spiritual stopper of good things to come, a melancholy builder and destroyer of faith. Barrier is of different design and formation. Enemy creates it to cause fear in our heart, but if you are in Christ, you have nothing to fear. Do not allow flesh to rule you, as it is written, **"For though we walk in the flesh, we do not war according to the flesh, for the weapons of our warfare are not of the flesh, but divinely powerful for the destruction of fortresses" 2 Corinthians 10:3-4.**

Satanic barrier is powerful; it restrains and blocks advancement of people. Barrier blocks your closeness with God. Barriers are created to cause you not to get what you want, or get it late. Barriers are created to hinder your success or blessings.

To ensure you are on the right path to prayer palace this book introduces you to power and benefits in faith building. Faith is a weapon that propels life to abundance. Family faith is what is believed will help you grow. A family with faith forges ahead and goes places. They excel in prayer as a family and a generation with bright future. Faith is a foundation to explore good things of life. Faith generates power. It gives strength to forge ahead and occupy mountain top.

You can't but experience strongholds of darkness in the race of life. This book gives insight to how satanic stronghold is built to demote life or pull someone down. Satan uses stronghold to oppress rather than to promote life. When we talk of stronghold, we mean spiritual not physical stronghold. The stronghold we fight is not physical but spiritual. **"The weapons we fight with are not the weapons of the world. On the contrary, they have divine power to demolish strongholds" 2 Corinthians 10:4-5.** The stronghold we fight is not the physical mountains before us but imaginable of it. It is no situation of taking into captivity enemy soldiers or persons, but bringing down enemy though.

For the fact that, powers may arise to alter, block or destroy a destiny, or family, you must arise and fight the battle in unison or intercede for the family. Prayer is the key to unlock your destiny. To open a locked door, you need the right key to open it. Without the right key, opportunities will be wasted and destiny rubbished. The very key you need depends on the lock. Wrong key means failure at hand. Here, you ask yourself which key I can use to open the door of my destiny. Your key may be prayer, songs of praise and worship to God, evangelism, speaking in tongues etc. This book teaches you that whichever key you discover will suite you, use it. But, prayer makes them work like fire.

This book also teaches about spiritual blindness, which is a condition individual or family face when they are unable to see God, or understand his message. A person who does not see God, does not know God. To people or family that is spiritually blind, spiritual things are meaningless. Such can make family reject God's Word because they can't understand the truth of the scripture

Above all, you will be introduced to how a family's health works to the glory of God. When your health is good and grow in the Word, you will burst into songs of joy. By this, the family grows in prayer and breaks every barrier against family growth. They will have nothing to fear, they grow and never shrink.

Here I declare, no weapon formed against you shall prosper, and you shall enjoy the heritage of the Lord. The book is yours buy it.

GOOD NEWS!!!

My audiobook is now available, to get one visit **acx.com** and search **"Tella Olayeri."**

Brethren, to be loaded and reloaded visit: *amazon.com/author/tellaolayeri* for a full spiritual sojourn for my books.

Thanks.

PREVIOUS PUBLICATIONS OF THE AUTHOR

1. <u>100% CONFESSIONS and PROPHECIES to Locate Helpers and helpers to locate you</u>
2. <u>1000 Prayer Points for Children Breakthrough</u>
3. <u>1010 (One Thousand and Ten) DREAMS and Interpretations</u>
4. <u>2000 Dangerous Prayer for First Born</u>
5. <u>365 DREAMS and INTERPRETATIONS</u>
6. <u>430 Prayers to Cancel Bad Dreams and Overcome Witchcraft Powers part one (DREAMS AND YOU Book 1)</u>
7. <u>430 Prayers to Claim Good Dreams and Overcome Witchcraft Powers part two (DREAMS AND YOU Book 2)</u>
8. <u>630 Acidic Prayers: With Missile Prayer for Speedy Breakthrough, Healing and Deliverance</u>
9. <u>650 DREAMS AND INTERPRETATIONS</u>
10. <u>700 Prayers to Clear Unemployment Out of Your Way</u>
11. <u>720 Missile Prayers that Silence Enemies: Prayers that Bring Peace and Rest</u>
12. <u>740 Rocket Prayers that Break Satanic Embargo</u>
13. <u>777 Deliverance Prayers for Healing and Breakthrough</u>
14. <u>800 Deliverance Prayer for Middle Born: Daily Devotional for Teen and Adult</u>

See all at: amazon.com/author/tellaolayeri

Table of Contents

CHAPTER 1

BREAKING WITCHCRAFT BARRIER AGAINST FAMILY GROWTH

Breaking witchcraft barrier is a tough spiritual assignment a family does. Witchcraft barrier is a tough nut to break, but God being on your side, you shall overcome it. Witchcraft barrier is a spiritual stopper of good things to come, a melancholy builder and destroyer of faith. Barrier is of different design and formation. Enemy creates it to cause fear in our heart, but if you are in Christ, you have nothing to fear. Do not allow flesh rule you, as it is written, **"For though we walk in the flesh, we do not war according to the flesh, for the weapons of our warfare are not of the flesh, but divinely powerful for the destruction of fortresses" 2 Corinthians 10:3-4.**

Satanic barrier is powerful; it restrains and blocks advancement of people. Barrier blocks your closeness with God. Barriers are created to cause you not to get what you want, or get it late. Barriers are created to hinder your success or blessings.

Every family must overcome mountains of the dark. There are mountains that may not allow you to move forward in life. Mountains are challenges of live. They constitute blockage, barrier and hindrance to souls. Mountains are not the physical things we see, but spiritual challenges that stand on our way as we journey in life. They cause us to be discouraged. They ensure we have a re-think of good plan we have. They frustrate us to challenge Satan and his agents because we are down on the floor. Satan never wants you or your family victorious in the race of life.

Barriers don't come to play overnight; there is power behind it. It is witchcraft power sourced from herbalist, witchcraft coven, evil altar, marine kingdom etc that eventually forms barrier. The source and power that operates it need to be known so that you may know the prayer to raise and the aggressiveness to apply. As a prayer warrior, you will rebuke the thought of enemies in crime or negative word spoken against you and your family. Speak positives to yourself and your family. Learn to say, "All attacks against my family is broken" "I shall not be in one spot of life" "Witchcraft barriers shall not hold me captive" etc.

Chains are created and used in the spirit to debar us from moving forward in life. Imagine you are chained to one spot in the physical, you are doomed, so it is in the spirit. You are going nowhere. Spiritual chains are unseen. They cause delay in decision making. When you observe you procrastinate in doing things know that spiritual chain is in operation.

The bible says, **"For you have not received the spirit of bondage again to fear. But you have received the spirit of adoption, whereby we cry, Abba, Father" Romans 8:15.** Our Lord did not create you in bondage, neither are you restricted to a place. Everywhere is yours, in as much you promote God's name. Fear should not be a word that should be found in your dictionary. With God everything is possible. The Lord is our peace; he never created us for bondage. It is written, **"For He Himself is our peace, who made both groups into one and broke down the barrier of the dividing wall". Ephesians 2:14.**

Your family must awake to prevail against every witchcraft stronghold, blockage and hindrance that demotes life. Command it to vanish at the sound of the great name of God. No power, erection or barrier can stay the test of time before God. The Lord is Great, Mighty than all things created, He is the creator of all things in the beginning, nothing created by us or any power can stir at the Almighty.

No matter the force, you must not be defeated or fall. The Lord is there to pick you up; whenever and wherever you and or your family may fall. Family growth is good, but you must be in one spirit to look unto God. Family prayer must concentrate on family growth, salvation and good work to succeed. Everyone in the family must know his salt. Everyone should be counseled in the Word and destiny development. No matter how big a ship is, rudder controls it. Parents must play prominent role in the lives of their children. In the manner we pray to God, hold your children in the palm of your hands and pray protective prayer upon their lives.

It is time we pray barrier breaking prayer that brings an end to every barrier that may stand on our way. Your family must break every existing barrier before broad way to breakthrough can be achieved. Every family should learn the act of warfare prayer, as you take your matter to God. With prayer and petition, tell God to remove the barrier. With prayer, break the barrier in pieces. Learn the act of using blood of Jesus to fight warfare prayer. By this, dissolve, break and destroy every barrier with power in the blood of Jesus. Arise like Elijah of the old, by calling fire and thunder to consume every barrier that proof stubborn to quit your way or family. Since there are forces and powers behind barriers, curse out every evil spirit that hinders your family. It is now time to break every chain and barrier that stands in your way and forge ahead in life.

PRAYER POINTS

1. I thank you Lord, for your love and protection upon my family in the name of Jesus.
2. I praise my God, who fills emptiness in my family with prosperity in the name of Jesus.
3. I thank my God, who breaks barrier of darkness raised against my family, in the name of Jesus.
4. I praise my God, Who is Light; that gives light to my family, in the name of Jesus.
5. O Lord, my family come towards you have mercy upon us in the name of Jesus.
6. O Lord, my family pleads for mercy and forgiveness, do it for us today, in the name of Jesus.

7. Lord Jesus, lay hand of forgiveness on everyone in my family today, in the name of Jesus.
8. O Lord, my family looks unto you, forgive us and bless us, in the name of Jesus.
9. I cover myself and family with pool blood of Jesus.
10. I plead blood of Jesus upon my family, in the name of Jesus.
11. Blood of Jesus, cleanse my family by your power and love, in the name of Jesus.
12. Blood of Jesus, be a hedge around my family in the name of Jesus.
13. Holy Ghost power, support my family to excel in the name of Jesus.
14. Holy Spirit, unite my family, in the name of Jesus.
15. Holy Spirit, be the Senior partner of my family, in the name of Jesus.
16. Holy Spirit, be my guide, be a light for my family in the name of Jesus.
17. Every dark fortress assign against my family be destroyed in the name of Jesus.
18. Satanic barriers, restraining my family to the Promised Land, I pull you down in the name of Jesus.

19. Satanic barrier, restraining my family to the Promised Land, I pull you down in the name of Jesus.
20. Powers that give satanic barrier support to disgrace my family expire and rise no more, in the name of Jesus.
21. Every plan of darkness to silence my family, scatter in the name of Jesus.
22. Angels of God; arise; scatter every work of darkness against my family in the name of Jesus.
23. Satanic barriers in my family life break to pieces in the name of Jesus.
24. I spray every dark barrier against me and my family with blood of Jesus, and destroy it, in the name of Jesus.
25. Thunder fire of God; destroy every dark barrier erected against my family in the name of Jesus.
26. Oh heaven, curse the powers that vow to stagnate my destiny in the name of Jesus.
27. Every child born in my family shall arise above evil barrier in the name of Jesus.
28. Every arrow of stagnation fired against my family backfire in the name of Jesus.
29. Every arrow of backwardness fired against my family, backfire, in the name of Jesus.

30. Every arrow of shame and disgrace fired against my family from the pit of hell backfire in the name of Jesus.
31. Every arrow of untimely death fired by neighbors against my family backfire, in the name of Jesus.
32. Every arrow fired to bury the destiny of my family, backfire to your sender in the name of Jesus.
33. Every arrow from the grave fired against my family, go back to your sender, in the name of Jesus.
34. Workers of iniquity in charge of my family problem die and rise no more in the name of Jesus.
35. My father and my God arise; destroy powers that vow my family will not excel, in the name of Jesus.
36. Satanic barrier, blocking my advancement and of my home, scatter, in the name of Jesus.
37. Every barrier, that blocks my family closeness to God, expire in the name of Jesus.
38. Every barrier causing me to lose my right, catch fire in the name of Jesus.
39. Every barrier, erected to put my family on a lost side, expire in the name of Jesus.

40. Powers that want my family to live from hand to mouth, expire, in the name of Jesus.
41. Spirit of late comer, assigned to make my family lose what is theirs, die and rise no more, in the name of Jesus.
42. O earth open, swallow every barrier on my way, in the name of Jesus.
43. My father and my God, destroy powers giving strength to barriers erected against my family, in the name of Jesus.
44. Weapons of darkness organized to destroy my family, backfire, and consume your owner, in the name of Jesus.
45. Character assassins, assigned to pull down my family, die in the name of Jesus.
46. Chain of darkness, assign for my family in the spirit, break in the name of Jesus.
47. Power that vow, my family is going nowhere, die, in the name of Jesus.
48. Spirit of procrastination dwelling in my life, come out and die, in the name of Jesus.
49. Every power, behind the barrier tormenting my family, expire, in the name of Jesus.
50. Witchdoctor, in charge of my family's case, be impotent, in the name of Jesus.
51. Evil altar, causing problem in my family, catch fire and roast to ashes, in the name of Jesus.

52. Marine powers, molesting my family in the spirit, expire, in the name of Jesus.

53. Every marine spirit, causing rise and fall in my family, expire, in the name of Jesus.

54. Powers camouflaging as friend but are enemy, be exposed and be disgraced, in the name of Jesus.

55. Spirit of bondage in my family, die and rise no more, in the name of Jesus.

56. O Lord, break down barrier of the dividing wall affecting my family, in the name of Jesus.

57. Every witchcraft stronghold, holding my family captive, catch fire and roast to ashes, in the name of Jesus.

58. Witchcraft blockages against my family lineage expire, in the name of Jesus.

59. O Lord, you are the creator of all things, let witchcraft barriers troubling my family expire today, in the name of Jesus.

60. Every mountain on my family way to success be pulled down in the name of Jesus.

61. Every mountain erected against my family, expire, in the name of Jesus.

62. Every mountain that vow my family shall not move forward, your time is up, clear away, in the name of Jesus.

63. My soul, reject discouragement to move forward in the name of Jesus.

64. Satan, you and your agents, leave my family alone, quit in the name of Jesus.

65. I receive staff of victory and march ahead in the name of Jesus.

66. Every barrier of any design or formation against my family, scatter in the name of Jesus.

67. Powers blocking my family breakthrough die, in the name of Jesus.

68. I smash the head of poverty troubling the growth of my family in the name of Jesus.

69. Powers assign against the finance of my family, die and rise no more, in the name of Jesus.

70. Every satanic barrier, become powerless in the name of Jesus.

71. Every yoke witchcraft barrier introduced to the life of my family break, in the name of Jesus.

72. I rebuke spirit of poverty dancing in the corridor of my family in the name of Jesus.

73. Every garment of failure assigned for my family, catch fire and roast to ashes, in the name of Jesus.

74. My family, reject financial burial assign for us, in the name of Jesus.

75. I rebuke spirit of devourer hunting my family, in the name of Jesus.

76. Barrier that locks the door of my family breakthrough, expire, in the name of Jesus.
77. Sword of fire, cut the head of power troubling me, in the name of Jesus.
78. Barrier causing demonic scarcity in my family, expire in the name of Jesus.
79. Evil re-arrangement caused by witchcraft barrier, scatter in the name of Jesus.
80. Witchcraft prophecy against my family, backfire, in the name of Jesus.
81. Every strongman or strongwoman in charge of my family's case, be exposed and be disgraced in the name of Jesus.
82. Every strange fire as a result of witchcraft barrier, quench in the name of Jesus.
83. O Lord, anoint the eyes of my family to see barriers and know what to do, in the name of Jesus.
84. O Lord, let harvest meet harvest in the life of my family, in the name of Jesus.
85. O Lord, lead everyone in my family to people that will bless them in the name of Jesus.
86. Anointing of excellence fall upon my family in the name of Jesus.
87. O Lord, dismantle any power working against my family destiny, in the name of Jesus.

88. O Lord, surprise my family with abundance of wealth, in the name of Jesus.
89. O Lord, enlarge the coast of my family, in the name of Jesus.
90. Power of resurrection come mightily upon my family and give us breakthrough, in the name of Jesus.
91. O Lord, turn my family to power breaker, in the name of Jesus.
92. My family; arise and shine, in the name of Jesus.
93. My family; turn every barrier to stepping stone to progress and breakthrough in the name of Jesus.
94. My family shall laugh and be grateful to God Almighty for His support to us, in the name of Jesus.
95. My family shall walk over challenges and problems stirring at us, in the name of Jesus.
96. My family shall not go to others to beg for food, in the name of Jesus.
97. My family shall move forward, not backward, in the name of Jesus.
98. All attackers against my family shall fail and rise no more, in the name of Jesus.

99. My family shall not be in one spot of life, we shall move forward by fire, in the name of Jesus.

100. Witchcraft barrier shall not hold my family captive, in the name of Jesus.

101. O Lord, accept our family prayer to grow and be in good health in the name of Jesus.

102. Today and forever more, O Lord, let my family lay hands in what will promote your name in Jesus name I pray. Amen

CHAPTER 2

O LORD BUILD THE FAITH OF MY FAMILY

Faith is a weapon that propels life to abundance. Family faith is what is believed will help you grow. A family with faith forges ahead and goes places. They excel in prayer as a family and a generation with bright future. Faith is a foundation to explore good things of life. Faith generates power. It gives strength to forge ahead and occupy mountain top.

The book of Hebrew, chapter eleven, verse one, says it all. **"Now faith is being sure of what we hope for and certain of what we do not see"**. Really, you don't see it, but have the picture in the heart. The picture of what you expect propels you to believe it is possible and achievable. You may have doubt along the line, but jettison it if it brings set back. You will excel if you have faith in what you do. Faith and works are like the light and heat of a candle; they cannot be separated. If you don't have what you do, and hope is lost, faith disappears.

A family must pursue faith with action, not only to pray and fold arms. No matter your faith, you must support it with action. Faith is not only act of counting millions of dollars in the nearest future, or build houses; or have educated children; it involves leaving old styles of life, like idolatry, but marry yourself to Jesus. Many stayed long in idolatry and lost faith. They believed they won't be accepted by Christ; past is past, today is today. It is today that Jesus needs, yesterday is gone, if you don't go back to it.

Father Abraham left his ancestral home as an infidel; but grow to be father of faith. The Israelites were not infidel in Egypt but never prayed. With faith Moses led the Israelites out of Egypt, crossed the Red Sea with faith, and with faith they occupied the Promised Land. The Saints of God are sealed inwardly with faith, but outwardly with good works. Until men have faith in Christ, their best services are but glorious sins. Faith justifies the person and works justify his faith.

It is time every family builds faith to occupy the portion of grace God have for them. A family must come to good works by faith and not to faith by good work. Faith comes first, and then work follows. Pray for faith to outshine work, yet good work with bountiful proceeds will follow. Faith is confidence in God's grace. Faith is so sure and certain that a family could stake its life on it a thousand times.

Faith is not an achievement; it is a gift. Yet it comes only through the hearing and study of the Word. May the Lord Almighty give your family the gift to build faith and excel. Let's go to hour of prayer.

PRAYER POINTS

1. I thank you Lord for your protection upon my family in the name of Jesus.
2. I thank you O Lord, for you shall build the faith of my family, in the name of Jesus.
3. O Lord, forgive my generation of the sins that deflates family faith in the name of Jesus.
4. O Lord, wear my family clothe of righteousness that builds faith in the name of Jesus.
5. O Lord, spread your hands of mercy and favour to my family to build our faith and be strong in the Lord in the name of Jesus
6. Lord Jesus, let your precious blood flow from the head to the toes of my family to build our faith in the Lord, in the name of Jesus

7. Lord Jesus, build the faith of my family with your precious blood that flows around us in the name of Jesus

8. Holy Ghost fire, take over the spiritual battle around my family and make our faith bold like lion in the name of Jesus

9. Holy Spirit Divine, strengthen the faith of my family to do exploit, in the name of Jesus.

10. My faith, bring abundance to me and my family, in the name of Jesus.

11. Tree of faith in my family, favor me to grow in the name of Jesus.

12. My family; arise and shine, to the glory of the Lord, in the name of Jesus.

13. Holy Spirit; baptize my family with prayer to excel and shine, in the name of Jesus.

14. Holy Spirit, baptize my family with multiple breakthroughs and shine, in the name of Jesus.

15. Strange foundation in my family working against my family, expire, in the name of Jesus.

16. Heavenly faith, come upon my family, in the name of Jesus.

17. O Lord, give me faith that will strengthen my family to forge ahead in the name of Jesus.

18. Spirit of wisdom; take over the lives of everyone in my family, in the name of Jesus.

19. Good things difficult for others to accomplish, my family shall do, in the name of Jesus.
20. Good future awaiting my family, come alive, in the name of Jesus.
21. Every arrow that kills faith fired against my family, backfire, in the name of Jesus.
22. Light of God, shine upon my family in the name of Jesus.
23. Father Abraham, left idolatry and follow God, O Lord, keep my family to you, in the name of Jesus.
24. O Lord, here I am, I present my family to you, accept us, in the name of Jesus.
25. Past is past, today is today, my family surrender to Christ today, in the name of Jesus.
26. Our past shall not rubbish today in my family, in the name of Jesus.
27. O Lord, give my family strength to grow in line with Father Abraham, in the name of Jesus.
28. O Lord, empower my family to occupy the Promised Land assigned for us in the spirit, in the name of Jesus.
29. My family, the Lord provides us garment of faith, everyone take yours and wear it, in the name of Jesus.
30. Colorful celebration, be the portion of my family in the name of Jesus.

31. Witch doctor assigned to kill my family faith, die and rise no more, in the name of Jesus.

32. O Lord, give my family position of grace, in the name of Jesus.

33. I am loaded with confidence of God, my family shall not scatter in the name of Jesus.

34. O Lord, give my family the zeal to pray and study the Word in the name of Jesus.

35. Habitation witchcraft in my family, I pull you down in the name of Jesus.

36. Every throne of darkness, raised against my family, be pulled down in the name of Jesus.

37. Witchcraft communication system raised against my family, catch fire and roast to ashes, in the name of Jesus.

38. Stubborn witchcraft power after my family, expire in the name of Jesus.

39. Every ritual targeted against my family, expire in the name of Jesus.

40. Every opposition against my family growth, scatter in the name of Jesus.

41. With faith, Abraham embarked on a journey he knew not, and was blessed, with faith my family shall not fail in the journey of life in the name of Jesus

42. With faith, Abraham had Isaac, my family shall not be childless, in the name of Jesus.

43. With faith, Abraham dug well until he met water, faith shall make my family dig deep to everlasting source of joy in the name of Jesus

44. With faith, Abraham dug well and found water; with faith my family shall not lack good things of life in the name of Jesus

45. With faith, Abraham dug well and found water, with faith my family shall get good result and good portion of life in the name of Jesus

46. With faith, father Abraham possessed the Canaan Land even after death, my family shall possess their inheritance in the name of Jesus

47. By faith, God created heaven and earth, and make us dominion over creation, my family shall not lose of God's creation in the name of Jesus

48. By faith Abraham build and occupy home of tents in a foreign land, my family shall build homes with foundation whose architect and builder is GOD in the name of Jesus

49. By faith, Abraham obeyed God to sacrifice his only son, Isaac, he passed the test and was blessed, my family shall not fail God's test in the name of Jesus

50. By faith, Isaac prayed to the Lord on behalf of his wife to bear children, God answered him,

children in my family shall not be barren, in the name of Jesus.

51. By faith, Isaac prayed for Jacob and his coast enlarged; by faith I prophesy greatness into the life of my family in the name of Jesus

52. By faith Jacob blessed his twelve children to achieve greatness, and it came to pass, our children shall move forward by fire in the name of Jesus

53. By faith Abel offered God better sacrifice than Cain did, and was commended as a righteous man, my family shall receive faith of righteousness in the name of Jesus

54. By faith, Enoch was taken to heaven, he never experienced death, by faith my family shall serve God with faith and seriousness; and make heaven in the name of Jesus

55. By faith Noah built the Ark to save lives of impending disaster, by faith my family shall know right from wrong and be blessed in the name of Jesus

56. By faith Noah, condemned the world and became heir of the righteous that came by faith, my family shall build faith to obey God in the name of Jesus

57. By faith, Moses parents hid him for three months after birth and was found out, and was

taken to the palace nursed by his mother, by faith my family shall locate helpers in the name of Jesus

58. By faith, Moses refused to be carried away with palace pleasure, for a short time, by faith my family shall not lose to sin in the name of Jesus

59. By faith, Moses left Egypt, he persevered in foreign land until God called him, my family shall build faith until God find's us out in the name of Jesus

60. By faith, Moses kept the Passover and the sprinkling of the blood, the children of Israel were saved, my family shall build faith to believe in God and be saved in the name of Jesus

61. By faith, Moses and the Israelites crossed the Red Sea and were saved, but the Egyptians lost out, my family shall build faith to cross every danger zone unhurt in the name of Jesus

62. By faith, Moses appeared before Pharaoh and eventually set the Israelites free, by faith my family shall defeat every Pharaoh in their life in the name of Jesus

63. Moses build faith in rescuing the Israelites, my family's faith shall set many free, in the name of Jesus.

64. By faith, Moses defeated enemies on their way to occupy Canaan Land, every occupant of my family's seat shall be unseated, in the name of Jesus.

65. By faith the wall of Jericho fell before Joshua and the Israelites, every Jericho wall before my family shall fall, in the name of Jesus.

66. By faith, the prostitute Rahab welcomed the spies and was saved, by faith my family shall not fall by enemies' sword in the name of Jesus

67. O Lord, build the faith of my family to sing songs of victory even before it happens, in the name of Jesus.

68. O Lord, build the faith of my family to count profit not loss before manifestation, in the name of Jesus.

69. O Lord, build the faith of my family to break every dark covenant holding us captive in the name of Jesus.

70. O Lord, build the faith of my family, to destroy powers standing at the gate of our breakthrough in the name of Jesus.

71. O Lord, build the faith of my family to break every chain of darkness fashioned against us, in the name of Jesus.

72. O Lord, build the faith of my family, to break every yoke of poverty in our lives, in the name of Jesus.

73. O Lord, build the faith of my family, to overcome serpentine powers assigned against us, in the name of Jesus.

74. O Lord, build the faith of my family, to overcome marine powers troubling our prosperity, in the name of Jesus.

75. O Lord, build the faith of my family, to attack and defeat enemy of our prosperity, in the name of Jesus.

76. O Lord, build the faith of my family to silence every monitoring power after our lives, in the name of Jesus.

77. O Lord, build the faith of my family to destroy every gadget of darkness fashioned against us, in the name of Jesus.

78. O Lord, build the faith of my family to grow and excel in the name of Jesus

79. O Lord, build the faith of my family, to fight and waste the wasters assign against us, in the name of Jesus.

80. O Lord, build the faith of my family to overcome eating in the dream in the name of Jesus.

81. O Lord, build the faith of my family against dark spirit children in the name of Jesus.
82. O Lord, build the faith of my family to overcome spirit of disgrace fashioned against us, in the name of Jesus.
83. O Lord, build the faith of my family, to overcome demonic influence, in the name of Jesus.
84. O Lord, build the faith of my family to overcome dream pollution, in the name of Jesus.
85. O Lord, build the faith of my family, to overcome every manner of satanic dream, in the name of Jesus.
86. O Lord, build the faith of my family to overcome demonic manipulation, in the name of Jesus.
87. O Lord, build the faith of my family to overcome fear that causes defeat in the name of Jesus.
88. O Lord, build the faith of my family to defeat opposition of darkness, in the name of Jesus.
89. O Lord, build the faith of my family to overcome spirit of backwardness, in the name of Jesus.

90. O Lord, build the faith of my family to recover what we lost to enemy in the dream, in the name of Jesus.

91. O Lord, build the faith of my family to excel in whatever we do, in the name of Jesus.

CHAPTER 3

O LORD PULL DOWN EVERY STRONGHOLD IN MY FAMILY

A stronghold can be a defensive structure or a place occupied by spiritual powers ready to molest victims. Satanic stronghold is built to demote life or pull someone down. Satan uses stronghold to oppress rather than to promote life. When we talk of stronghold, we mean spiritual not physical stronghold.

The stronghold we fight is not physical but spiritual. **"The weapons we fight with are not the weapons of the world. On the contrary, they have divine power to demolish strongholds" 2 Corinthians 10:4-5.** The stronghold we fight is not the physical mountains before us but imaginable of it. It is no situation of taking into captivity enemy soldiers or persons, but bringing down enemy though.

A stronghold becomes a threat, only if there are enemy soldiers inside. The spirit of God wants us to capture any demonic stronghold that holds us captive. It is when you subdue or capture enemy stronghold, Holy Spirit is permitted in the life. Stronghold is battle between Satan and Holy Spirit.

Strongholds are captured by people who are willing to fight with zeal. One thing to know about stronghold is, it is a place not a person. It is the place occupied by satanic agents or Satan, and or, a place occupied by Holy Spirit.

The person in a stronghold can be your enemy or your friend. Your stronghold can be a place of comfort or a safe place. A spiritual stronghold is a habitual pattern of thought, build into ones thought life. Satan and his agents want to capture the minds of people; the mind is the citadel of the soul. If you want abundant life and peace that God promised us, you must let his spirit capture the stronghold of Satan.

There is battle to fight if you want to pull down stronghold of Satan in a family. Satanic stronghold was built over the years, even before you were born. To pull it down you must be filled with Holy Spirit. You have battle to fight. A stronghold is a way of thinking and feelings that developed to a personality in a person. It develops to act and react, to control or be controlled. What occupies the place dictates whether it is positive; Holy Spirit or negative, satanic.

To intercede for the family, you must identify the type of stronghold you fight. You don't pray in amiss. Know your target and fire your shots! To break witchcraft barriers against family growth is not a mere battle. It is a hard nut that needs wisdom, fire prayer, intelligence, braveness and boldness. Identify the barrier, pull it down and break it to pieces so that it rises no more. If you know such barrier needs to be set on fire in the spirit do so. Burn it to ashes with prayer in the spirit with heavenly command.

As a brave soldier, ready for battle to stand in gap for the family, and or, you need to call them together for prayer, make sure you do it in one accord. Family prayer is good, as two heads in spirit is better than one.

PRAYER POINTS

1. I thank you Lord for your protection over my family, from the stronghold of the enemy in the name of Jesus.
2. I thank you Lord, for you shall not allow stronghold of the enemy to enslave my family in the name of Jesus.

3. O Lord, have mercy upon my family, in the name of Jesus.

4. O Lord, let your love and favour, swallow sins that counts against my family in the name of Jesus.

5. Blood of Jesus, breakdown every stronghold troubling the soul of my family, in the name of Jesus.

6. I cover my family with blood of Jesus.

7. Let blood of Jesus, flow round my family for safety, in the name of Jesus.

8. Holy Spirit, lay hands of protection upon my family, in the name of Jesus.

9. Holy Ghost Power; set my family free from stronghold of darkness, in the name of Jesus.

10. Every stronghold tormenting my family; be pulled down in the name of Jesus.

11. Every stronghold that surrounds my family; be pulled down in the name of Jesus.

12. O Lord, give my family wing of great eagle to escape the stronghold of deadly powers that surround us in the name of Jesus.

13. O Lord, give my family wing of eagle to fly high in the midst of enemy, and never be pulled down, in the name of Jesus.

14. Every stronghold around my family, I pull you down in the name of Jesus.

15. Every stronghold built by neighbors around us in order to torment my family, catch fire and roast to ashes in the name of Jesus.
16. Every stronghold built by neighbors where my children/sibling live, to destroy them, be pulled down, in the name of Jesus.
17. Evil plantation in the garden of my family, catch fire and roast to ashes, in the name of Jesus.
18. Every idol of my father's house tormenting my family, die in the name of Jesus.
19. Every idol of my mother's house troubling my family, die and rise no more, in the name of Jesus.
20. Satanic stronghold boasting against my family's prosperity, scatter in the name of Jesus.
21. Satan, my family is not your victim, surrender and leave us alone, in the name of Jesus.
22. Divine weapon in my hand demolish every stronghold captivating my family, in the name of Jesus.
23. Every mountain boasting against my family's destiny, shut up, expire, in the name of Jesus.
24. Every wicked thought of the enemy against my family, backfire in the name of Jesus.

25. Dark soldiers that create road block against my family, your time is up, die, in the name of Jesus.
26. Enemy soldier in the stronghold after my family, die and rise no more, in the name of Jesus.
27. Demonic stronghold, I capture you and pull you down, in the name of Jesus.
28. Every stronghold that hold my family captive, I strangulate you, die, in the name of Jesus.
29. Enemy stronghold die, Holy Spirit, occupy my life, in the name of Jesus.
30. O Lord, crown my family destiny with crown of breakthrough, in the name of Jesus.
31. I run to stronghold and fortress of God and I am save, in the name of Jesus.
32. O Lord, let your fortress be my family fortress, in the name of Jesus.
33. My mind you are released from the captivity of the enemy in the name of Jesus.
34. Stronghold of Satan in my family, planning to carry out evil, expire, in the name of Jesus.
35. Evil thoughts in my life, I jettison you in the name of Jesus.
36. Stronghold of untimely death, deliberating on when to announce death in my family, be pulled down, expire, in the name of Jesus.

37. Stronghold of poverty in my family, die, in the name of Jesus.
38. Stronghold of bareness in my family, die, in the name of Jesus.
39. Stronghold of promise and fail directing the affairs of my family, die, in the name of Jesus.
40. Every witchcraft activity in my environment against my family, scatter, in the name of Jesus.
41. Every arrow of wickedness, backfire, in the name of Jesus.
42. Every camp of witchcraft that gather against me, scatter, in the name of Jesus.
43. Every root of witchcraft in my family, wither, in the name of Jesus.
44. Enemies of my family, walk out of our environment in the name of Jesus.
45. O Lord, deliver my family from the sword of wickedness, in the name of Jesus.
46. O Lord, make haste to help me, in the name of Jesus.
47. Stronghold of darkness challenging God, expire in the name of Jesus.
48. Evil forest that stands as stronghold against my family, dry up, catch fire and roast to ashes, in the name of Jesus.
49. Evil rock that stands as stronghold against my family, break to pieces in the name of Jesus.

50. Altar of darkness that represents stronghold in my family's life, I pull you down, catch fire and roast to ashes in the name of Jesus.
51. Evil tree dedicated by powers of darkness against the life of my family, be uprooted, fall down by fire in the name of Jesus.
52. Evil River that flows against my family's destiny, dry up in the name of Jesus.
53. Evil lake that hold my family in bondage, dry up, in the name of Jesus.
54. Every limitation in the life of my family, as a result of stronghold power, expire, in the name of Jesus.
55. Evil land that represent stronghold troubling the life of my family, die in the name of Jesus.
56. Every charm and amulets in the house where any of my family lives, holding them captive, lose your hold upon them in the name of Jesus.
57. Demonic utterances that captivate my family's destiny, backfire, in the name of Jesus.
58. Occult power binding my family to poverty, expire, in the name of Jesus.
59. Any power, using the sand to control the life of my family, you are a failure, die, in the name of Jesus.

60.Every strange leg roaming about to destroy my family's reputation, paralyze, in the name of Jesus.

61.Landlord spirit tormenting my family wherever they live, expire and be powerless over them, in the name of Jesus.

62.Every stronghold attacking my family career, expire, in the name of Jesus.

63.Every stronghold that want my family to occupy the valley, die, in the name of Jesus.

64.Powers tormenting my family in the dream, expire in the name of Jesus.

65.Stronghold powers assign to chain my children down to one spot, expire in the name of Jesus.

66.Network of darkness; helping powers of darkness to operate freely in the lives of my family, catch fire and roast to ashes in the name of Jesus.

67.Occult powers that represent stronghold in the lives of my family expire, in the name of Jesus.

68.Grave yard spirit, killing people at will in my lineage, we are not your candidate; expire, in the name of Jesus.

69.Every strongman or woman attacking my family be silenced, in the name of Jesus.

70. Every stronghold assigned to introduce frustration into the life of my family, scatter, in the name of Jesus.

71. Every stronghold assigned to introduce limitation into the life of my family, scatter, in the name of Jesus.

72. Every stronghold assigned to introduce stagnation into the life of my family, scatter, in the name of Jesus.

73. O Lord my father, do not allow the labour of my family be in vain, in the name of Jesus.

74. Every stronghold causing tough time in the life of my family, die, in the name of Jesus.

75. Stronghold powers that capture the glory of my family, release them now, in the name of Jesus.

76. Every stronghold renewing problem upon problem in the life of my family, die, in the name of Jesus.

77. Faculty of darkness; in the life of my family, disappear, in the name of Jesus.

78. Familiar spirits, troubling the destiny of my family, die, in the name of Jesus.

79. No weapon fashioned against my family shall prosper, in the name of Jesus.

80. Stronghold of darkness, disappear in the life of my family, in the name of Jesus.

81. My family, give every stronghold around you knockout blow, in the name of Jesus.
82. My family; surrender your life to Christ and win every battle that comes our way, in the name of Jesus.
83. My family, every giant attacking us shall die, in the name of Jesus.
84. My family shall not be trees without fruits, in the name of Jesus.
85. My family, overcome every foaming sea against our destiny in the name of Jesus.
86. My family, be prayerful and powerful to overcome every stronghold on our way, in the name of Jesus.
87. My family, every stronghold shall be a walkover for us, in the name of Jesus.
88. My family shall bury every stronghold assign to cause tears in our lives, in the name of Jesus.

CHAPTER 4

THE DESTINY OF MY FAMILY SHALL NOT BE RUBBISHED

Family destiny is synonymous to family tree. Your family is a branch of your generational family tree; whether you are a man or a woman. Family destiny is a generational thing. Destiny is how you live your life or what you make of life, your destiny is close to your handwork. Destiny is your future or the pre-ordained path of your life. Destiny is what keeps everything moving. Destiny is what generates the motivation to create, to establish, to explore and to fulfill.

When a barrier is created along the line, it means destiny is about to be rubbished. Damage can be done this way, to a destiny in the spirit. A destiny can be converted to rag, it makes one to be rejected anywhere he goes. Helpers detest you, while life becomes unbearable. Rag in the spirit can demote you and your work. It gives Mr. Failure opportunity to slaughter such destiny.

The vehicles of many families have been stolen. They don't know where they are going or coming from. They are confused. At this point, enemies re-arrange their destiny and scatter there plans.

Enemy can program against your destiny and that of the family at large. By this, flying stars are high jacked or killed. Altars of darkness are mounted against destiny to frustrate it. Enemy can go further, to cook a destiny with evil cauldron in order to manipulate it. Destiny swallowers go on rampage to cause havoc. Destiny thieves steal destiny to stop you from making it in life. These and many others are the hand work of the wicked.

Really, powers may arise to alter, block or destroy a destiny or of a family. You must arise and fight the battle in unison or intercede for the family. Prayer is the key to unlock your destiny. To open a locked door, you need the right key to open it. Without the right key, opportunities will be wasted and destiny rubbished. The very key you need depends on the lock. Wrong key means failure at hand. Here, you ask yourself which key I can use to open the door of my destiny. Your key may be prayer, songs of praise and worship to God, evangelism, speaking in tongues etc. Whichever key you discover that will suite you, use it. But, prayer makes them work like fire.

Take the matter of your family to God. He is a destiny changer. **"He raises the poor from the dust and lifts the needy from the ash heap; he**

seats them with princes, with the princes of their people. He settles the barren woman in her home as a happy mother of children. Praise the LORD". Psalm 113:7-9.

I say again, take the matter of your family to God; come to Zion, so that your destiny can be re-branded, re-covered, re-strengthened etc. You can do this by taking the following prayer steps.

1. Speak against anything spoken against the destiny of your family in the heavenlies.
2. Pull down satanic altar erected against the destiny of your family.
3. Pray that the destiny of the family shall not suffer affliction.
4. Pronounce judgment against evil altar erected against the destiny of the family.
5. Repair, every damage done to your family's destiny in prayer.
6. Rebuke and resist power assigned to change the destiny of your family.
7. Stand against every right of the enemy to rob the destiny of your family.
8. Pray that the desire of the enemy against your family shall not be granted in the heavenlies.
9. Pray that every darkness designed for your family shall not stand.

10. Pray that every evil deposit on your family destiny shall expire.
11. Pray that every foothold of the enemy upon your family destiny should be erased.
12. Pray that every incantation, spell, jinx and ritual shall backfire.
13. Pray for workers of iniquity to depart from your family.

These and many other prayers should be prayed to deliver your family destiny from the captivity of the enemy. Your prayer and the family are weapons you must not joke with. It is time to pray and break every witchcraft barrier raised against the growth of your family.

PRAYER POINTS

1. I thank you Lord, for your protection upon my family, in the name of Jesus.
2. I thank you my Lord, for keeping my family alive, in the name of Jesus.
3. O Lord my God, empty evil thought in the life of my family, in the name of Jesus.
4. O Lord, lay hands of forgiveness upon my family so that sin shall find no place in us, in the name of Jesus.

5. I soak the destiny of my family in the pool blood of Jesus.

6. Blood of Jesus, purge my family of evil deposit, in the name of Jesus.

7. Holy Spirit, re-brand my family to excel in the name of Jesus.

8. Holy Ghost Fire, arise let your fire burn all that is not holy in the life of my family, in the name of Jesus.

9. O Lord, listen to my petition, help me out today for my family, in the name of Jesus.

10. O Lord, silence every enemy of my family that is against our prayer, in the name of Jesus.

11. Every stronghold of the wicked assigned to destroy the destiny of my family, be pulled down in the name of Jesus.

12. Every network of the wicked assign against the progress of my family, break, in the name of Jesus.

13. Every darkness that surrounds the destiny of my family, be swallowed by light of God, in the name of Jesus.

14. Every demon programmed into my family, in order to rubbish our destiny, expire, in the name of Jesus.

15. Every satanic cage designed to rubbish my family, break to pieces, in the name of Jesus.

16. Spirit of lawlessness quit the life of my family in the name of Jesus.
17. Every enemy of my family's miracle, expire, in the name of Jesus.
18. My family tree shall not wither, in the name of Jesus.
19. My family tree shall not be uprooted in the name of Jesus.
20. Strangers occupying my family tree; fall down and die, in the name of Jesus.
21. Powers assigned to rubbish my family and make us poor; die, in the name of Jesus.
22. Powers assigned to put my family to shame, expire and rise no more in the name of Jesus.
23. Powers that rise up against my lineage; die, in the name of Jesus.
24. Powers ordained to stop my family marching forward, your time is up, expire, in the name of Jesus.
25. O Lord, plant seed of motivation in my family to create new ideas of prosperity, in the name of Jesus.
26. O Lord, establish my family on progressive foundation that will announce my family to the world, in the name of Jesus.
27. O Lord, plant in my family spirit to explore and make wealth, in the name of Jesus.

28. Barriers created by enemy to rubbish my destiny, break, in the name of Jesus.
29. Every damage done to my family's destiny, be healed, in the name of Jesus.
30. Evil arrow fired to scatter the destiny of my family, backfire in the name of Jesus.
31. Powers on assignment to turn my destiny to rag, shall fail in the name of Jesus.
32. Spirit of rejection, in charge of my destiny, die, in the name of Jesus.
33. Mr. Failure, assigned to slaughter my destiny, your time is up, die, in the name of Jesus.
34. Powers in charge of my family destiny to rob it of her glory die, in the name of Jesus.
35. Spirit transport of my family destiny, shall not be destroyed, in the name of Jesus.
36. Power assigned to steal the transport of my family destiny, meet double failure, in the name of Jesus.
37. Every wicked program against my family destiny, scatter, in the name of Jesus.
38. Destiny star killers after the stars of my family, die, in the name of Jesus.
39. Star hijacker after the stars of my family, be disgraced and be defeated, in the name of Jesus.

40. Altar of darkness assigned against my destiny catch fire and roast to ashes, in the name of Jesus.
41. Powers cooking the glory of my family destiny, your time is up, die, in the name of Jesus.
42. Evil pot enemies are using to cook the glory of my family destiny, break in the name of Jesus.
43. Every power ordained to alter my family destiny, expire, in the name of Jesus.
44. O Lord, bless me with prayer key to recover what my family lost in the past, in the name of Jesus.
45. O Lord, give me key of breakthrough that will turn the life of my family around, in the name of Jesus.
46. O Lord, give me right key to open doors of breakthrough of my family under satanic watch, in the name of Jesus.
47. My father and my God, make my family matter in my place of birth, in the name of Jesus.
48. Every adversary tormenting my family in the spirit, die in the name of Jesus.
49. Every dark prison waiting to captivate my family, catch fire, and roast to ashes, in the name of Jesus.
50. Every witchcraft judgment against my family, backfire, in the name of Jesus.

51. Load of darkness apportioned my family in the evil world, catch fire and roast to ashes, in the name of Jesus.

52. Siege of darkness, hear the word of the Lord, scatter, in the name of Jesus.

53. Violent angels of God, arise, slap the face of powers dragging the name of my family in the mud, in the name of Jesus.

54. Workers of iniquity depart from the corridor of my family, in the name of Jesus.

55. Every incantation spoken to affect and destroy my family destiny, backfire, in the name of Jesus.

56. Every ritual carried out against my family destiny backfire, in the name of Jesus.

57. Every foothold of the enemy upon my family destiny, expire, in the name of Jesus.

58. Every deposit on my family deposit, dry up and die, in the name of Jesus.

59. Every dark design of the enemy for my family, scatter and be nullified in the name of Jesus.

60. Every desire of the enemy for my family, scatter, in the name of Jesus.

61. Witchcraft robber after my family, die, in the name of Jesus.

62. I rebuke and resist any power assign to change my family destiny to nothing, in the name of Jesus.

63. Powers assigned to weaken the destiny of my family die in the name of Jesus.

64. O Lord, silence powers that want my family to be dragged on the floor, in the name of Jesus.

65. Arrow of affliction fired against my family, backfire in the name of Jesus.

66. I speak woe to every witchcraft altar erected to rubbish and silence my family in the name of Jesus.

67. O Lord, let me give testimony of great things you do in my family in the name of Jesus.

68. Songs and praises of the Lord shall not depart from my mouth, in the name of Jesus.

69. Satanic altar, standing as medium of attack against my family, catch fire and roast to ashes, in the name of Jesus.

70. Powers that trouble the Israel of my family, be troubled in the name of Jesus.

71. Every rebellion against the destiny of my family, scatter, in the name of Jesus.

72. Any power assign to harvest good things in the life of my family in order to rubbish them, die in the name of Jesus.

73. Idol of my father's house supervising activities of my family to harm us, die in the name of Jesus.
74. Ancestral battles that refuse to let my family go, expire in the name of Jesus.
75. Powers troubling my family in the dream, expire, in the name of Jesus.
76. Every arrow of darkness fired at my family to rubbish our destiny, backfire in the name of Jesus.
77. Yokes and covenant of diseases, waiting to rubbish my family, break in the name of Jesus.
78. Thou power that trouble the peace of my family, enough is enough, expire, in the name of Jesus.
79. Evil program against my family, scatter in the name of Jesus.
80. Woe to every troubler of my family destiny, in the name of Jesus.
81. Garment of darkness assigned to rubbish the destiny of my family, catch fire and roast to ashes in the name of Jesus.
82. Wasters assigned against my family be wasted in the name of Jesus.
83. Prophecy of bareness and childlessness against my family, backfire in the name of Jesus.

84. Ancestral warrior of Satan that vows my family shall not make it, die, in the name of Jesus.
85. Powers in charge of my environment attacking my family, die, in the name of Jesus.
86. Powers chanting on sand to devalue my family destiny die, in the name of Jesus.
87. I rebuke every cycle of backwardness in the destiny of my family, in the name of Jesus.
88. I rebuke every spirit of stagnancy in the destiny of my family, in the name of Jesus.
89. I rebuke every prosperity terminator assign to rubbish the destiny of my family, in the name of Jesus.
90. O Lord, keep the lives of everyone in my family save from danger, in the name of Jesus.
91. Powers, assign to drink the blood of my family member, die, in the name of Jesus.
92. Eaters of flesh and drinkers of blood planning to rubbish my family in the spirit, die, in the name of Jesus.
93. Every dark prayer, against my family backfire, in the name of Jesus.
94. Every dark prophecy, against my family destiny, backfire in the name of Jesus.
95. Every dark gathering, against my family, scatter, in the name of Jesus.

96. Thou destiny of people in my family, become untouchable for enemy to rubbish, in the name of Jesus.
97. O Lord, re-new the memory of my family, to excel in what they do, in the name of Jesus.
98. Holy Ghost Power, undress my family of evil garment, in the name of Jesus.
99. Holy Ghost Power, secure my family defense; against powers assigned to rubbish us, in the name of Jesus.
100. Every serpent and scorpion, against my family destiny, die, in the name of Jesus.
101. My family, experience rain of divine immunity upon our life, in the name of Jesus.
102. My family, be covered by shadow of the Living God, in the name of Jesus.
103. My family, no power shall rubbish you, receive first class support today, in the name of Jesus.
104. My family, by the power of the Living God, I command your destiny to jump out of the pit of debt, in the name of Jesus.
105. My family, what you labour to get shall not be stolen by spiritual robbers, in the name of Jesus.
106. My family, the Lord shall make you the head and not the tail, in the name of Jesus.

107. My family, the Lord shall deposit greatness in our lives in the name of Jesus.

108. My family, the anointing of success and fruitfulness shall locate you by fire, in the name of Jesus.

109. My family, the Lord shall break and scatter every obstacle on our way to success, in the name of Jesus.

110. My family, resist and reject every killer disease assign to rubbish us, in the name of Jesus.

111. By the power of the Living God, none of my family shall die or be rubbished, in the name of Jesus.

CHAPTER 5

SPIRITUAL BLINDNESS IN MY FAMILY IS OVER

"My people are destroyed from lack of knowledge" Hosea 4:6. It is spiritual blindness that makes one or his/her family lack knowledge. If you seek the face of God in what you lay hands upon, your path will receive light and you will never stumble. Spiritual blindness is a spiritual disease. It kills and demotes destiny making it easy for enemy to register your family name in the book of failure. There is a key Satan gives to those who are blind in the spirit. It is key of backwardness. It is the key that yields other elements of degradation, such as, anger, failure, demotion, stagnation, jealousy, envy, cruelty, etc. Spiritual blindness is a sure way to hell fire. It makes you prayer less as you won't know what to pray about.

Spiritual blindness is a condition that individual or family has when they are unable to see God, or understand his message. A person who does not see God, does not know God. To people or family that is spiritually blind, spiritual things are meaningless. Such can make family reject God's

Word because they can't understand the truth of the scripture.

Family must pray for spiritual sight so that God may reign in their lives. It is when you have God's sight; you have hope or reign with God, or God reign in you. Spiritual blindness makes you fall into Satan's trap. Your family can be easily trapped with bait and fall.

Let's look at what Apostle Paul said in **2 Corinthians 4:4. "The god of this age has blind the minds of unbelievers, so that they cannot see the light of the gospel of the glory of Christ, who is the image of God."** When family goes astray from following Christ, they are blind. They see the things of the world and forget about the gospel that brings salvation to soul which is the gateway to heaven. Thus, spiritual blindness can make family lose heaven. Paul refers to Satan as the "god of this age (world)" Satan will definitely tempt you, but pray you don't fall, neither should it be the portion of your family. The problem with men is, we easily succumb to Satan's scheme, even in the Garden! The Garden of Eden, tells how quick human being can be blinded by worthless things of the earth. The weapon of Satan is deceitful and crafty.

The truth is, we must remain in light if we want to overcome darkness and be spiritually alert. We must open our spiritual eyes to understand the Word and the work of God. We must pray to remove veil that makes us dwell in the valley of blindness. Let's pray to have deep understanding of the Word and stop satanic harassment.

PRAYER POINTS

1. I thank you Lord for you shall visit my family with power today, in the name of Jesus.
2. I thank you Lord, for you shall put an end to spiritual blindness in the life of my family in the name of Jesus.
3. Lord Jesus, have mercy upon my family in the name of Jesus.
4. Lord Jesus, by your power forgive my family the sins we commit in the name of Jesus.
5. I cover my family with blood of Jesus.
6. Blood of Jesus, purge my family of satanic impurity in the name of Jesus.
7. Holy Spirit, lay hands of good vision upon my family, in the name of Jesus.
8. Holy Ghost Fire, purge my family blood from evil inheritance, in the name of Jesus.

9. Satanic deposit troubling the vision of my family, die in the name of Jesus.

10. O Lord, open the spiritual eyes of my family, in the name of Jesus.

11. O Lord, bind and destroy wicked demons polluting dream and vision of my family, in the name of Jesus.

12. O Lord, give my family spiritual power to operate with sharp spiritual eyes that cannot be deceived, in the name of Jesus.

13. O Lord, break every covenant of infirmity in my lineage that is affecting my family, in the name of Jesus.

14. O Lord, destroy every generational bondage of spiritual blindness in my family affecting my children, in the name of Jesus.

15. O Lord, break the chain of transferred spiritual blindness affecting my family, in the name of Jesus.

16. O Lord, fill me and my family with knowledge and understanding in the name of Jesus.

17. Every arrow of blindness fired against my family backfire, in the name of Jesus.

18. Where others fail, my family shall not fail, in the name of Jesus.

19. Every pit dug for my sake or any member of my family, shall consume the digger, in the name of Jesus.
20. Light of God, shine upon my family in the name of Jesus.
21. Spiritual disease in my life and of any member of my family; receive deliverance, in the name of Jesus.
22. Demoting power troubling my family, expire and rise no more in the name of Jesus.
23. Evil register that has my name and that of my family, catch fire and roast to ashes, in the name of Jesus.
24. Every key of backwardness given to me in the dream I reject you in the name of Jesus.
25. Spirit of anger assigned to work against my family salvation, expire in the name of Jesus.
26. Veil of darkness, covering my family, I pull you off, in the name of Jesus.
27. Veil of darkness, keeping my family in the valley, I tear you to pieces, in the name of Jesus.
28. Arrow of stagnation fired against my family, backfire in the name of Jesus.
29. Road of hell fire, opened to my family, close, and open no more, in the name of Jesus.

30. Spiritual blindness making my family to count loss, expire in the name of Jesus.
31. Spiritual blindness, that makes helpers turn against my family, expire, in the name of Jesus.
32. Spiritual blindness, that turn my family to slaves in the spirit, expire, in the name of Jesus.
33. Spiritual blindness that sow seed of prayerlessness in my family, expire in the name of Jesus.
34. O Lord, let my family finds you and know you, in the name of Jesus.
35. O Lord, let me and my family understand the Word and do what it entails, in the name of Jesus.
36. My family shall not live in darkness in the name of Jesus.
37. Arrow of darkness fired to make my family occupy bottomless pit, shall fail in the name of Jesus.
38. O Lord, reign in my family in the name of Jesus.
39. O Lord, give my family spiritual sight and light in the name of Jesus.
40. Every satanic trap set to catch me and my family, catch your owner in the name of Jesus.
41. Owner of evil load, carry your load, in the name of Jesus.

42. Things of the world shall not blindfold me against God in the name of Jesus.
43. My family shall not go astray from the Lord, in the name of Jesus.
44. Satan, my family is not your candidate, quit our lives in the name of Jesus.
45. Oh, heaven, take control of my family, smile to us, let us be victorious, in the name of Jesus.
46. Power to overcome darkness come upon my family in the name of Jesus.
47. Every hardship associated with spiritual blindness in my family, break in the name of Jesus.
48. Every power, that pursued my parents, and is now pursuing me, hands up and die, in the name of Jesus.
49. I fire back every witchcraft arrow fired against my family in the name of Jesus.
50. I fire back every arrow of spiritual blindness fired against my family in the name of Jesus.
51. Any power, assigned to plant cataract in the eyes of my family, die in the name of Jesus.
52. Every generational curse of blindness affecting my family break, in the name of Jesus.
53. I speak against evil power of my father's house that wants my family to be spiritually blind, in the name of Jesus.

54. I speak against evil power of my mother's house that attacks the vision of my family, in the name of Jesus.
55. I speak against evil power of my In-law's house that vows my family shall be spiritually blind, in the name of Jesus.
56. Strange powers using sickness to pursue my family die in the name of Jesus.
57. Every arrow fired from witchdoctor, against the spirituality of my family growth backfire, in the name of Jesus.
58. Every idol of my father's house, loose your hold upon the life of my family, in the name of Jesus.
59. Every evil power that vow to take away spiritual vision God endowed my family, die, in the name of Jesus.
60. Every strongman of my father's house waging war of spiritual blindness against my family, die, in the name of Jesus.
61. Every evil command against my family's vision, expire in the name of Jesus.
62. I speak woe against ancestral power with evil intention to silence my family, in the name of Jesus.
63. Every blood of darkness speaking against my family, dry up in the name of Jesus.

64. Wicked agenda, against my family, break in the name of Jesus.

65. Spiritual shrine, causing spiritual blindness in my lineage, expire and rise no more, in the name of Jesus.

66. Evil consequence of idolatry affecting my family vision, scatter, in the name of Jesus.

67. Everything hidden from my family in the spirit, be plain before us in the name of Jesus.

68. Anything my family ate or swallowed causing spiritual blindness in their lives, expire now, in the name of Jesus.

69. Cotton of darkness, spread in the face of my family, catch fire and roast to ashes, in the name of Jesus.

70. Garment of darkness in my family, causing spiritual blindness, catch fire and roast to ashes, in the name of Jesus.

71. Evil altar with evil role in the life of my family, I pull you down in the name of Jesus.

72. Bitter water of blindness troubling my family vision, dry up, in the name of Jesus.

73. Powers assign to capture and destroy the star of my family, your time is up, die in the name of Jesus.

74. Arrows of spiritual blindness, that originate idolatry in my family, loose your hold upon my family, in the name of Jesus.
75. Voice of darkness, assigned to take my family to the grave, be silenced in the name of Jesus.
76. O Lord, give my family the spirit of revelation and wisdom, in the name of Jesus.
77. O Lord, make the inner eyes of my family see deep to things of the spirit, in the name of Jesus.
78. O Lord, remove spiritual cataract from the eyes of my family, in the name of Jesus.
79. Evil veil in the eyes of my family, catch fire and roast to ashes in the name of Jesus.
80. Every strongman that vow to deal with my family, die in the name of Jesus.
81. Cloud of darkness that cover my family, clear away in the name of Jesus.
82. Power to read and understand the star, fall upon my family in the name of Jesus.
83. Light of God, shine upon the life of my family, and remove every darkness militating against them, in the name of Jesus.
84. Every harsh weather, affecting the spirit of my family, clear away in the name of Jesus.

85. Attacks of the enemy are over, my family, enjoy and swim in rivers of deliverance in the name of Jesus.
86. Blood of Jesus, wash the face of my family, in the name of Jesus.
87. Heavenly sight, come mightily upon my family, in the name of Jesus.
88. My family, be guided by angels of God, from all troubles of life, in the name of Jesus.
89. My family whether the enemy like it or not, receive deliverance from the grip of the enemy in the name of Jesus.
90. My family, your day of joy has come, arise and fly high like the eagle, in the name of Jesus.
91. My family, receive power from heaven and be set free from spiritual blindness, in the name of Jesus.

CHAPTER 6

GOOD HEALTH SHALL BE THE PORTION OF MY FAMILY

It is said, health is wealth. A healthy family in Christ is a healthy family for paradise. Every family must strive hard to be spiritually and physically healthy. Good health frees the mind to serve God. The body is the temple of God, and so, must be sound to serve God. Good health is synonymous to laughter and joy. Joyful heart praises God, knows God and worship God.

Good health will make you soar on wings like eagles, you will run and not grow weary, you will walk and not be faint. You will become new and sharp, ready to carry out activities of the day. The Lord our Redeemer, shall redeem you for great exploit.

A healthy family, that grows in the Word never lack. They burst into songs and shout for joy. The family grows in prayer and breaks every barrier against family growth. They will have nothing to fear, they grow and never shrink. No weapon forged against them prosper, they enjoy the heritage of the Lord.

The under listed Bible passages; attest to God's wish for us as His children. You will reap good health, joy, good provision, breakthrough and love of God.

3 John 1:2

2. Dear friend, I pray that you may enjoy good health and that all may go well with you, even as your soul is getting along well.

Proverbs 17:2

22. A cheerful heart is good medicine, but a crushed spirit dries up the bones.

Proverbs 31:17

17. She sets about her work vigorously; her arms are strong for her tasks.

Jeremiah 33:6

6. Nevertheless, I will bring health and healing to it; I will heal my people and will let them enjoy abundant peace and security.

Acts 27:34

34. Now I urge you to take some food. You need it to survive. Not one of you will lose a single hair from his head."

Exodus 23:25

25. Worship the LORD your God, and his blessing will be on your food and water. I will take away sickness from among you,

Proverbs 3:7-8

7. Do not be wise in your own eyes; fear the LORD and shun evil.

8. This will bring health to your body and nourishment to your bones.

Proverbs 12:25

25. Anxiety weighs down the heart, but a kind word cheers it up.

Proverbs 16:24

24. Gracious words are a honeycomb, sweet to the soul and healing to the bones.

James 5:14-15

14. Is anyone among you sick? Let them call the elders of the church to pray over them and anoint them with oil in the name of the Lord.

15. And the prayer offered in faith will make the sick person well; the Lord will raise them up. If they have sinned, they will be forgiven.

Jeremiah 17:14

14. Heal me, LORD, and I will be healed; save me and I will be saved, for you are the one I praise.

Malachi 4:2

2. But for you who revere my name, the sun of righteousness will rise with healing in its rays. And you will go out and frolic like well-fed calves.

Revelation 21:4

4. 'He will wipe every tear from their eyes. There will be no more death' or mourning or crying or pain, for the old order of things has passed away."

Isaiah 53:5

5. But he was pierced for our transgressions, he was crushed for our iniquities; the punishment that brought us peace was on him, and by his wounds we are healed.

Psalm 147:3

3. He heals the brokenhearted and binds up their wounds.

Proverbs 3:8

8. This will bring health to your body and nourishment to your bones.

Deuteronomy 7:15

15. The LORD will keep you free from every disease. He will not inflict on you the horrible diseases you knew in Egypt, but he will inflict them on all who hate you.

Jeremiah 30:17

17. But I will restore you to health and heal your wounds,' declares the LORD, 'because you are called an outcast, Zion for whom no one cares.'

Luke 9:11

11. But the crowds learned about it and followed him. He welcomed them and spoke to them about the kingdom of God, and healed those who needed healing.

<u>Ezekiel 47:12</u>

12. Fruit trees of all kinds will grow on both banks of the river. Their leaves will not wither, nor will their fruit fail. Every month they will bear fruit, because the water from the sanctuary flows to them. Their fruit will serve for food and their leaves for healing.

<u>Isaiah 58:14</u>

14. Then you will find your joy in the LORD, and I will cause you to ride in triumph on the heights of the land and to feast on the inheritance of your father Jacob." For the mouth of the LORD has spoken.

PRAYER POINTS

1. I thank you Lord that my family are alive and will be in good health in the name of Jesus.
2. I thank God, for his love and mercy for my family, in the name of Jesus.
3. Lord Jesus, lay hand of forgiveness, upon my family in the name of Jesus.
4. Lord Jesus, let your love and forgiveness be permanent in the lives of my family in the name of Jesus.
5. Blood of Jesus, purge my family of sickness and disease, in the name of Jesus.

6. Blood of Jesus, cleanse my family of health impurity, in the name of Jesus.
7. Holy Spirit, guide my family from health danger, in the name of Jesus.
8. Holy Spirit, lay hands of healing upon my family in the name of Jesus.
9. Holy Spirit, cast out, evil agents assigned against my family, in the name of Jesus.
10. My family health, improve by fire in the name of Jesus.
11. O Lord, let the root of infirmity planted by witchcraft powers in my family dry up, in the name of Jesus.
12. O Lord, let my family enjoy good health so that all may go well with us, in the name of Jesus.
13. O Lord, give my family a cheerful heart to praise you in the name of Jesus.
14. O Lord, heal my body and my family with heavenly medicine in the name of Jesus.
15. O Lord, let every organ in the body of everyone in my family be healthy and vigorous to carry out daily tasks in the name of Jesus.
16. O Lord, give my family good health with abundant peace and security in the name of Jesus.
17. None of my family shall lose a single hair from our head in the name of Jesus.

18. O Lord, bless our daily food and water for good health, in the name of Jesus.
19. Every bone of my family's body be nourished by the power of the living God, in the name of Jesus.
20. Kind words that nourish the heart, flow in my family as heritage in the name of Jesus.
21. O Lord, anoint my head with heavenly oil of healing in the name of Jesus.
22. O Lord, raise everyone that is sick my family up, let them be of good health, in the name of Jesus.
23. O Lord, heal my family and we shall be healed, save us, and we shall be saved, in the name of Jesus.
24. Every arrow of death fired against my family, backfire to sender, my God shall make me safe, in the name of Jesus.
25. O Lord, bind up every wound we suffer in my family in the name of Jesus.
26. O Lord, keep my family free from every disease, in the name of Jesus.
27. My family shall not be outcast, in the name of Jesus.
28. Every covenant with sickness and disease break in the name of Jesus.

29. Every wind of sickness, blow back to your sender, in the name of Jesus.

30. Every snare of sickness against my family, expire, in the name of Jesus.

31. Every plantation of sickness and disease in my family, wither and die in the name of Jesus.

32. O Lord; release Rivers of life upon my family in the name of Jesus.

33. Every agenda of darkness for my life, scatter in the name of Jesus.

34. O Lord, guide the footsteps of everyone in my family to good health, in the name of Jesus.

35. Every ancient door holding my family captive, break to pieces, in the name of Jesus.

36. Every cloud of uncertainty over my family health, clear away in the name of Jesus.

37. O Lord, build around my family protective hedge of fire, in the name of Jesus.

38. Bank blood of Satan, my family blood is not your portion, catch fire and burn to ashes, in the name of Jesus.

39. I curse every sickness and disease hunting my family, in the name of Jesus.

40. Inherited sickness in my lineage, expire in the name of Jesus.

41. Witchcraft prostitute, in the blood of my family, die in the name of Jesus.

42. Witchcraft sponsored disease, assigned to trouble my family, your time is up, expire in the name of Jesus.
43. Embargo placed upon the health of my family, break in the name of Jesus.
44. Missionary of darkness, assigned to commission the destiny of my family to bad health, die, in the name of Jesus.
45. Every satanic appointment with death, break in the name of Jesus.
46. Every witchcraft sponsored disease targeted at my family backfire, in the name of Jesus.
47. Foundational problem causing bad health in my family, expire, in the name of Jesus.
48. Witchcraft altar sponsoring sickness in the life of my family, catch fire and roast to ashes, in the name of Jesus.
49. Slow killers after the health of my family, die, in the name of Jesus.
50. Every arrow of insanity, fired against my family, backfire, in the name of Jesus.
51. Every arrow fired to kill helpers of my family, backfire, in the name of Jesus.
52. Every arrow of sickness and disease fired against my family, backfire, in the name of Jesus.

53. Every arrow fired to stockpile evil deposit in my family, backfire, in the name of Jesus.

54. Every arrow fired that introduce evil load in the life of my family, backfire, in the name of Jesus.

55. Witchcraft padlock that padlocked the health of my family, break to pieces in the name of Jesus.

56. Every witchcraft burial affecting the health of my family expire, in the name of Jesus.

57. Refuse of darkness, adding bad health to my family's life, catch fire and roast to ashes, in the name of Jesus.

58. Sickness inheritance in the life of my family break in the name of Jesus.

59. Strong room of darkness harboring my family's wealth, I pull you down, scatter, in the name of Jesus.

60. Witchcraft kingdom celebrating my family's bad health, scatter, in the name of Jesus.

61. Negative influence against my family health, scatter, in the name of Jesus.

62. The health of my family buried in the dark world, be reversed to good healh in the name of Jesus.

63. Marine blood bank dedicated in the spirit to collect my family blood, catch fire in the name of Jesus.

64. Every poison of darkness, troubling the health of my family, expire, in the name of Jesus.
65. Every arrow from pit of hell assigned to destroy and paralyze my family backfire in the name of Jesus.
66. Every battle in the life of my family, scatter, in the name of Jesus.
67. Old serpent attacking the health of my family, your time is up, die, in the name of Jesus.
68. Powers cooking the destiny of my family to cause bad health die, in the name of Jesus.
69. Every arrow of darkness fired against the backbone of my family, backfire, in the name of Jesus.
70. Every arrow fired against the organ of my family members, backfire, in the name of Jesus.
71. Every dark arrow fired into the eyes of my family members, backfire, in the name of Jesus.
72. Every dark arrow fired against the health of my family, backfire, in the name of Jesus.
73. Every dark arrow fired against my family's leg, backfire, in the name of Jesus.
74. Every dark arrow fired against the hands of my family members, backfire, in the name of Jesus.
75. Any arrow fired into any part of my family members, backfire in the name of Jesus.

76. Every arrow of memory failure fired against my family members brain backfire, in the name of Jesus.

77. O Lord, let my family receive touch of healing in their private organ, in the name of Jesus.

78. O Lord, let my family receive touch of healing . in the head, in the name of Jesus.

79. O Lord, let my family receive touch of healing in the hands, in the name of Jesus.

80. O Lord, let my family receive touch of healing in the womb and stomach, in the name of Jesus.

81. O Lord, let my family receive touch of healing in the legs, in the name of Jesus.

82. O Lord, let my family receive touch of healing in the mouth, in the name of Jesus.

83. O Lord, let my family receive touch of healing in the eyes, in the name of Jesus.

84. O Lord, give my family clean bill of health, in the name of Jesus.

85. Health hazards as a result of placenta witchcraft attack in my family expire in the name of Jesus.

86. The health of my family shall not deteriorate, in the name of Jesus.

87. O Lord, break the backbone of sickness in the life of my family, in the name of Jesus.

88. I speak against every lineage infirmity in my lineage that may trouble my family, in the name of Jesus.

89. I speak against sickness agenda of evil powers for my family, in the name of Jesus.

YOU HAVE BATTLES TO WIN
TRY THESE BOOKS

1. COMMAND THE DAY: DAILY PRAYER BOOK

Each day of the week is loaded with meanings and divine assurance. God did not create each day of the week for the fun of it. Blessings, success, gifts, resources, hopes, portfolios, duties, rights, prophecies, warnings and challenges, are loaded in each day.

Do you know the language, command or decree you can use to claim what belongs to you in each day of the week? Do you know in Christendom, Monday can be equated to one of the days of creation in Genesis chapter one? Do you know creation lasted for six days and God rested on the seventh day? What day of the week can Christian equate as the first day of the week, if we follow Christian calendar? What day can we call day seven?

This book shall give insight to these questions. It shall explain how you can command each day of the week according to creation in the book of Genesis chapter one.

Above all, you shall exercise your right and claim what is hidden in each day of the week.
Check for this in <u>COMMAND THE DAY: DAILY PRAYER BOOK</u>

2. <u>PRAYER TO REMEMBER DREAMS</u>

A lot of people are passing through this spiritual epidemic on a daily basis. Their dream life is epileptic, having no ability to remember all dreams they dream, or sometimes forget everything entirely. This is nothing but spiritual havoc you need to erase from your spiritual record.
The answer to every form of spiritual blackout caused by spiritual erasers is found in, <u>PRAYER TO REMEMBER DREAMS</u>

3. <u>100% CONFESSIONS AND PROPHECIES TO LOCATE HELPERS AND HELPERS TO LOCATE YOU</u>

This is a wonderful book on confessions and prophecies to locate helpers and helpers to locate you. It is a prayer book loaded with over two thousand (2,000) prayer points.

The book unravels how to locate unknown helpers, prayers to arrest mind of helpers and prayers for manifestation after encounter with helpers.

4. ANOINTING FOR ELEVENTH HOUR HELP: HOPE AND HELP FOR YOUR TURBULENT TIMES

This book tells much of what to do at injury hour called eleventh hour. When you read and use this book as prescribed fear shall vanish in your life when pursuing a project, career or contract.

5. PRAYER TO LOCATE HELPERS AND HELPERS TO LOCATE YOU

Our divine helper is God. He created us to be together and be of help to one another. In the midst of no help we lost out, ending our journey in the wilderness.

There are keys assign to open right doors of life. You need right key to locate your helpers. Enough is enough; of suffering in silence.

With this book, you shall locate your helpers while your helpers shall locate you.

6. FIRE FOR FIRE PART ONE: (PRAYER BOOK BOOK 1)

This prayer book is fast at answering spiritual problems. It is a bulldozer prayer book, full of prayers all through. It is highly recommended for night vigil. Testimonies are pouring in daily from users of this book across the world!

7. PRAYER FOR FRUIT OF THE WOMB: EXPECTING MOTHERS

This prayer book is children magnet. By faith and believe in God Almighty, as soon as you use this book open doors to child bearing shall be yours. Amen

8. PRAYER FOR PREGNANT WOMEN: WITH ALL CHRISTIAN NAMES AND MEANINGS

This is a spiritual prayer book loaded with prayers of solution for pregnant women. As soon as you take in, the prayers you shall pray from day one of conception to the day of delivery are written in this book.

9. <u>**WARFARE IN THE OFFICE: PRAYER TO SILENCE TOUGH TIMES IN OFFICE**</u>

It is high time you pray prayers of power must change hands in office. Use this book and liberate yourself from every form of office yoke.

10. <u>**MY MARRIAGE SHALL NOT BREAK: THE SECRET TO LOVE AND MARRIAGE THAT LASTS**</u>

Marriage is corner piece of life, happiness and joy. You need to hold it tight and guide it from wicked intruders and destroyer of homes.

11. <u>**VICTORY OVER SATANIC HOUSE PART ONE: RIDDING YOUR HOME OF SPIRITUAL DARKNESS**</u>

Are you a tenant, Land lord bombarded left and right, front and back by wicked people around you?
With this book you shall be liberated from the hooks of the enemy.

12. <u>**DICTIONARY OF DREAMS: THE DREAM INTERPRETATION**</u>

DICTIONARY WITH SYMBOLS, SIGNS, AND MEANINGS

This is a must book for every home. It gives accurate details to about **10,000 (Ten thousand) dreams and interpretations,** written in alphabetical order for quick reference and easy digestion. The book portrays spiritual revelations with sound prophetic guidelines. It is loaded with Biblical references and violent prayers.

Ask for yours today.

For Further Enquiries Contact
**THE AUTHOR
EVANGELIST TELLA OLAYERI
P.O. Box 1872 Shomolu Lagos.
Tel: 08023583168**

FROM AUTHOR'S DESK

BEFORE YOU GO

Hello,

Thank you for purchasing this book. Would you consider posting a review about this book? In addition to providing feedback and arousing others into Christ's bosom, reviews can help other customers to know about the book.

Please take a minute to leave a review on this book.

I would appreciate that!

Thank you in advance, for your review and your patronage!!

Feel free to drop us your prayer request. We will join faith with you and God's power will be released in your life and issue in question.

http://tellaolayeri.com/prayerrequest.php

NOTE: You can get all my books from my website http://tellaolayeri.com

GOOD NEWS!!!

My audiobook is now available, to get one visit acx.com and search **"Tella Olayeri."**

Brethren, to be loaded and reloaded visit: amazon.com/author/tellaolayeri for a full spiritual sojourn for my books.

Thanks.